KT-455-737

The counts of Andechs acquired the settlement on the right banks of the Inn in 1180 and named it after the bridge over the river, Inns-Bruck. In 1248 the city passed over into the hands of the counts of Tyrol. The Habsburgs moved their court from Meran to Innsbruck. That was the start of an enormously fruitful building period. The city "skyline" is dominated by the **towers of the Baroque Cathedral (Dom)** and the late **Gothic City Tower (Stadtturm),** but towering above all are the grandiose mountains (Bettelwurf, right).

The part of the city on the left bank of the Inn was where the old market of the Andechs counts was located before 1180. Viewed from the right bank of the Inn, the late Gothic and Baroque gabled houses with their colorful facades are especially picturesque against the scenic mountain background of the snow-covered "Nordkette".

"If I were to win 1000 Imperial Thaler in the lottery, I would take a friend and fly to Tirol," wrote Hans Christian Anderson in 1871. Like many modern holiday makers, Anderson felt the strong attraction of the grandiose mountains of Tyrol. The mountains cover a full 7/8 of the surface of Tyrol. No wonder that already before 1271 it was known in old script as "Lant im Gepirg" ("Land in the Mountains"). The entire course of Tyrolean history has felt the impact of this geographical reality.

Both the height of the mountains and the extended ice age created unfavorable conditions for plants, animals and people to thrive in. Consequently, the settlement of Tirol began relatively late, historically speaking. Nevertheless, a group of bone spearheads discovered in the Kaiser Valley near Kufstein goes back as far as 30,000 B.C.

A sensational discovery in the Oetz Valley proved beyond doubt that the early inhabitants of Tyrol spent at least part of their time in the great heights. Buried in glacial ice on the Hauslab saddle, the 5200-year old mummified body of a man was found, probably a shepherd. He is now fondly called "Oetzi" by the local inhabitants.

While the mountain heights became the major factor in the slow formation of the geological landscape, the factor which had the most enduring importance on Tyrol's history was its location as the supreme "land of passes" through the Alps. Nowhere else is it as easy to cross the Alps as over the Brenner and Reschen Passes.

The Romans were already aware of this when Field Commanders Drusus and Tiberius conquered the alpine regions and added them to the empire in 15 B.C. The major part of modern Tyrol became part of the Roman province of Rhaetia, while East Tyrol was assigned to the Roman province of Noricum. In Aguntum, East Tyrol, the only Roman city on Tirolean soil, city walls, houses, baths and the foundations of an early Christian basilica were discovered. During the nearly 500 years of Roman dominion, the Rhaetian populace was superficially romanized. Their language - Rhaeto-Roman - can still be heard in isolated areas of South Tyrol's Gardena Valley, and was spoken in parts of the upper Inn Valley well into the 19th century.

After the destruction of the Roman empire, the Bavarians undertook a systematic settlement of the land. A great many names of rivers and towns go back to the "Rajuwarian" land seizure in the 6th and 7th centuries.

With the coronation of Charlemagne in Rome in the year 800, the Holy Roman Empire was born in Europe. Since imperial coronations were always performed by the Pope, every Frankish (and later on, German) king had to cross the Alps to reach Rome. Thus, it was essential for every ruler to have the alpine region securely under control, or at least in the cooperative hands of a friendly ruler. As the bishops of Brixen were considered especially loyal to the king, they were granted governing powers over the region north of Brixen, the Inn Valley (north of the Brenner) and later the Puster Valley. As Church dignitaries, they were not permitted to engage in either the military defense of the land or court jurisdiction of serious cases, so turned a part of their worldly power over to local aristocratic governors. The counts of Tyrol, who derived their name from the proud fortress above Meran, proved themselves the most capable of these protectors. As a result, the land became known as the Dominion of the Counts of Tyrol as of the 13th century.

After the Counts of Tyrol died out, their inheritance fell into the hands of the Counts of Görz (Gorizia). One of the most capable members of this dynasty, which was to prove so important to Tyrolean history, was Meinhard II. He founded the monastery at Stams, which later was to serve as the burial vault for Tyrolean sovereigns. With great determination, Meinhard II. expanded his dominion, promoted commerce and transportation, created new administrative bodies, and drew up the body of Tyrolean law.

From the Romanesque period, which lasted into the 14th century in Tyrol, there are but few works still in existence, since they were so often replaced by Gothic works in the 15th century. As worthy examples of small Romanesque country churches, the ones in Nösslach am Brenner, Matrei in East Tyrol and Kals am Grossglockner can be cited.

Meinhards granddaughter Margarete Maultasch was the last countess from the Görz-Tyrol line. After the death of her son, Margarete Maultasch handed the County of Tyrol over to the Habsburg dukes Rudolf, Albrecht and Leopold of Austria, thereby attaching the greatest part of Tyrol to Austria. The Puster Valley, East Tyrol, and the regions east of Ziller joined later. Tyrol came under the dominion of Leopold's line of the Habsburg family. Leopold's son, Friedrich IV., the famous Duke "Friedl of the Empty Purse" was without doubt the most popular Tyrolean prince outside of Emperor Maximilian. In his war against the rebellious landed aristocracy, the Tyrolean peasants stuck loyally to him. When, in 1423, the Tyrolean estates met together as a parliament for the first time, not only aristocrats and bourgeois, but also peasants were represented. The imperial residence was transferred from Meran to Innsbruck, which was strategically located on the crucial east-west axis of the Habsburgs. Shrewd financial policy, competent government and the beginning of mining operations in Tyrol made it possible for Friedrich, once the duke with an empty purse, to leave behind a great inheritance to his son Sigmund, "Rich of Coin" as he came to be called. Under his regency, the mining of silver in Tyrol increased and the mint foundry in Hall was built.

In the 15th century, Tyrolean construction underwent a great boom. Partly due to the wealth created by mining, great late Gothic cathedrals (Hall, Absam, Schwaz, Seefeld, Imst) were built, as well as fine bourgeois homes outfitted with galleries, oriel windows and crenelated gables (Innsbruck, Rattenberg, Hall). Typical secular architecture of the time are the City Hall (Rathaus), Burg Hasegg and the Mint Tower (Münzerturm) in Hall, and the City Tower (Stadtturm) in Innsbruck.

Sigmund's opulent lifestyle and, to an even greater extent, his unhappy war with Venice led to the mortgaging of the Tyrolean silver mines. In the end, Sigmund was forced to abdicate. His cousin Maximilian, already King of the Germans and three years later to become Emperor, succeeded him in 1490. Innsbruck remained his preferred residence, which he beautified with the Golden Roof ("Goldenes Dachl") and his magnificent tomb in the Imperial Church (Hofkirche). While the Golden Roof doubtless is the most radiant example of late Gothic secular architecture in Innsbruck, the tombs in the Innsbruck Hofkirche have to be assigned to the Renaissance. One encounters Maximilian elsewhere in Tirol as well: after the acquisition of Kufstein, Rattenberg and Kitzbühel, he had the fortress of Kufstein erected and built the citadel of Rattenberg into a fortress. Maximilian was an enthusiastic hunter and fisherman and ventured into the high mountains as well. The hunting and fishing annals ("Tiroler Jagdbuch" and "Tiroler Fischereibuch"), based on the personal records of Maximilian and illustrated by court painter Jörg Kölderer, bear witness to this activity. After having inherited the Puster Valley and East Tyrol, the borders of Tirol were drawn which - with the exception of the Ziller Valley, which joined Tirol in 1817 - were to remain unchanged for 400 years.

After Maximilian's death, the fate of Tyrol was determined by the Reformation, Counter-reformation and the Peasants' War. Not until Ferdinand II., a son of Emperor Ferdinand I., did Tyrol again have its own prince. Ferdinand lived in morganatic marriage with the daughter of the patrician family from Augsburg, Philippine Welser. Since she was excluded from official court life, Ferdinand had Ambras Castle near Innsbruck rebuilt in Renaissance style for her. Here, where she was able to create her own court, she became a legend for her gentleness. Ferdinand was one of the most cultivated men of his time, with a profound sensitivity to art. His "Ambras Collection" is the first of the great art collections of the Habsburgs. After 1665, this line of the Habsburgs was extinguished: Tyrol was drawn more and more into the centralized official government of the Habsburgs, especially throughout the 18th century. The Innsbruck Imperial Palace (Hofburg), which Empress Maria Theresia rebuilt in the "modern" baroque style of the day, bears visible witness to this.

The Baroque period lent a new burst of energy to construction. In the middle of the 17th century, a doctor named Hippolyt Guarinoni built the Servitenkirche in Volders in the lower Inn Valley. Soon thereafter the Gumpps, an Innsbruck family of builders, began three generations of construction activity in Innsbruck and Tyrol. From them we have the Jesuit Church (Jesuitenkirche), the Mariahilfkirche, the Wilten monastery church (Stiftskirche), the city palaces of Taxis, Sarnthein and Trapp, and the old city hall of Innsbruck. Especially important architecturally is the Baroque reconstruction of the Cistercian monastery church in Stams, in the upper Inn Valley.

Ever since Maximilian, Tyrol has had a special defense status: Tyroleans could not be drafted into military service for wars beyond their borders. However, they were obliged to defend their own land themselves, for which purpose the peasants were permitted to bear arms. The well-prepared veteran reserves which developed as a result of this provision had already succeeded in warding off the Bavarians. The Tyrolean Rifle Company became legendary for its battles against the French. In the course of the Napoleonic Wars, Tyrol and Vorarlberg were handed over to the French ally, Bavaria. But Bavaria was a hated master in Tyrol, due to its religious policies. When Austria declared war on France and Bavaria in 1805, the resistance movement in Tyrol was born. The fact that a bunch of armed Tyrolean peasants managed to beat the conquering French army was like something out of a fairy tale. This aspect was only further enhanced by the appearance of the imposing figure of Andreas Hofer and his eventual execution in Mantua. This mythical yet historically real man is still an integral part of Tyrol's culture today.

In the second half of the 19th century, Tyrol joined the European-wide network of railways. It was during this time that the charms of the mountains were discovered. The Alps were opened as a region of leisure activity of high restorative value, and soon alpine clubs and organizations were founded. Tourism was born, in time to become a valuable and lucrative source of revenue.

World War I forced Tyrol to defend its homeland once again. Even though Tyrol succeeded in defending its southern borders against the attacks of Italy, the Treaty of Versailles in 1919 ceded South Tyrol to Italy.

The depression following the war and the long absence of German tourists (upon whom the economy had come to depend) with the introduction of the 1000-Mark Barrier almost brought ruin upon Tyrol. Then, after World War II., Tyrol experienced an unusually strong economic upsurge, compared to the rest of Austria. However, the building of the Inn Valley and Brenner highways, as well as the ever-increasing numbers of tourists, all placed a burden on the delicate balance of nature and the Tyroleans' treasured environment which now require a new perspective on any future development of this region.

The state capital **Innsbruck** lies in the wide bowl on the Inn River, where the Wipp Valley begins
southern route toward the Brenner Pass, the classic route across the Alps from Germany to Italy. Innsbru
(population about 130,000) is the cultural, administrative and economic centre of the state and its or
largish city.

The **old town (Altstadt)** was originally encircled by city walls and a moat. The streets Marktgraben, Burggraben and Herrengasse followed the course of the moat. The **Golden Roof (Goldene Dachl),** on the main facade of the citadel erected in 1420, has become the emblem of the city of Innsbruck. Nikolaus Thüring the Elder designed the magnificent roofed balcony with oriel-window on the occasion of Maximilian's second marriage, to Bianca Maria Sforza of Milan, in 1494.

The **Maria-Theresien-Straße** cuts straight through the inner town, right to the edge of the old town. The **Anna Column (Annasäule)** was erected in 1703 as a sign of gratitude for fending off the Bavarian invasion. The **Triumphal Arch (Triumphpforte)** was built as a memorial of the wedding of Maria Theresia's second son, Leopold, to the Infanta Maria Ludovica in Innsbruck in 1765.

The **Imperial Church (Hofkirche)**
was built by Ferdinand I. in 1553-63
for the special purpose of housing
the tomb of Emperor Maximilian. The
portal reveals the strong influence of
the late Renaissance. The **tomb of
Emperor Maximilian** occupies the
greater part of the nave, flanked on
all sides by the impressive, larger-
than-life bronze statues. For that
reason, the church is known as the
"Black Fellows" Church in local dia-
lect. The work which was begun
during the lifetime of Maximilian
remained unfinished. The Emperor
died in Wiener Neustadt and was
buried there.

he picturesque location of **Ambras Castle** in the middle of a gorgeous park above the city makes a visit ere a rewarding experience, further enhanced by the art treasures, weapons collection and the public oms of the castle. Archduke Ferdinand II. had the medieval castle rebuilt into the largest and most agnificent Renaissance castle in Austria for his wife Philippine Welser.

nother lovely walk leads up to Bergisel, with its Kaiserjägermuseum and the **Olympic ski jump.** The lympic flame has been ignited twice here. From the plateau one enjoys a unique view out over the whole ty and the surrounding mountains.

Wild headdresses and carved wooden masks: the **Mardi Gras,** pre-fasting season, as in the Muller ritual celebrations in the villages between Innsbruck and Hall, can be hard work. In the pictures you can see the village of **Thaur** with the Stubai glacier in the background, and house motifs in **Absam.**

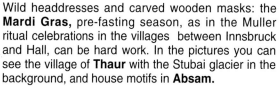

out 10 kilometers down-
eam from Innsbruck is
old salt-mining city of
l. The almost completely
act **old town (Altstadt),**
of late Gothic houses
m the 15th and 16th cen-
es is a unique memorial
city architecture of the
ddle Ages. The **Mint**
wer (Münzerturm) from
15th century is the
dmark of the town. It
ongs to Burg Hasegg,
ch served as safeguard
he salt works, the bridge
r the Inn and the boat
rs at river's edge and
housed the minting
ndry. In the center, the
er of the **Damenstifts-**
che rises, behind it the
erheiligenkirche (All
nts Church). On the up-
r city square, the **city**
ish church of St. Niko-
s with its late Gothic
ve stands in stark con-
t to the Baroque tower.

East of Hall, right on the highway, is one of the most interesting Gothic buildings in Tyrol, the **Karlskirche.**
It was designed in the middle of the 17th century by a doctor, Dr. Hippolyt Guarinoni, in early Baroque style.

n a hill you can see **Burg Friedberg** with its mighty 13th century dungeon. Its present shape has mained unchanged since Maximilian's time. The Knights' Room (Rittersaal) is ornamented with late Gothic urals.

ne **southeastern ramparts** are the perfect spot for a wonderful spring walk, where you can gaze over the wer-covered meadows up to the snowy slopes of the **Karwendel** chain of mountains.

15

South of the famous **Europabrücke on the Brenner highway,** the road turns off into the high alpine Stubai Valley. Behind **Telfes,** the steep rocky walls of the Kalkkögl rise toward the sky.

western ramparts also have their charm. The picturesque village centre of **Mutters** is dominated by the Gothic parish church tower, which Peter Anich equipped with a sun dial. Mutters is also well known for especially profuse flowers, mounted in boxes on the balconies of the houses.

Fulpmes is the main village of
Stubai Valley. In the background,
peaks of the Stubai glacier unfol
spectacular stage setting surrounds
three villages of Mieders, Telfes
Fulpmes.

The **Stubai Valley** was discovered early by tourists. Besides its beautiful mountain scenery, it also has had its own narrow-gauge railway since 1904, which runs from the city of Innsbruck through lovely pine forests on the way to Fulpmes.

Toward the end of the valley is the idyllic hamlet of **Krössbach**, with its one inn. On the private road to the glacier cablecar, you come very near to the grand **Grawa Waterfall**, a protected nature reserve.

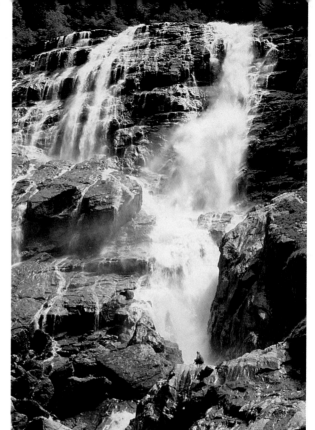

The **Wilde Freiger**, 3418 meters high, is one of the most frequently climbed mountains in the main chain of the Alps because of its beautiful and (relatively) easy summit routes.

The **Stubai Valley Glacier Cablecar (Stubaitaler Gletscherbahn)** with the Schaufelspitze (3333m) in th
background draws guests all year round to a ski area 12 square kilometers large.

he valley which leads from Innsbruck via the
renner to South Tyrol is called the **Wipptal**. The
d road followed the Roman route. In **Matrei**, with
lovely bourgeois houses from the 15th to 17th
nturies, transit traffic was the pulsing lifeline of
e village until the building of the Brenner
ghway.

In the **side valleys of the Wipptal**, such as the Navis, Schmirn, Valser, Obernberg and Gschnitz Valleys, you still find primeval Tirol. In the picture on the left, the hay hut on the green meadows contrasts starkly with the snowy **Sagwand**.

The snow-covered slopes of the **Olperer** reflect down on the Valser Valley even in the height of summer.

In Nößlach, the **St. Jakob Chapel (Kapelle St. Jakob)**, one of the few Romanesque structures in Tirol.

Swarovski's Crystal Worlds in **Wattens** attract hundreds of thousands of visitors annually. Artist **André Heller** has created in the belly of a water-spewing giant a fantastic world all around the theme of crystal.

Approximately 25 kilometers of Innsbruck in the lower Inn Va is the "silver city" of **Schwaz**. was the leading mining town i of Europe in the 15th and 16th turies. At that time, it was also second largest city in Austria, after Vienna, with as many as 4 miners living here. Because of many miners, the **Stadtpfarrki** was enlarged to contain chancels, one for the citizens one reserved for the miners.

At the **observation mine**, one gets a glimpse into the mining operations of olden days. The electric mining gallery-railway leads 800 meters into the depths to the old Sigmund-mine, excavated in 1491.

The **Freundsberg Castle** stands guard on a little hill, 170 meters above the valley floor. It is the family castle of the Tyrolean aristocratic family of the same name, having been acquired and rebuilt by Duke Sigmund "Rich-in-Coin" in the 15th century.

On the other side of the valley is somewhat isolated **St. Georg berg**. This was one of the most portant pilgrimmage churches Europe in the Middle Ages. Its P dates back to 1415. One reaches Georgenberg via the romantic Wo klamm, through the most beau wild brook path in Tyrol.

Between Jenbach and Stans, in geous surroundings on its own mc tain slope, is **Castle Tratzberg** has survived the centuries well. magnificent rooms with their mast marble and woodwork permi wonderful glimpse into the lifestyl the Gothic-to-Renaissance period.

The high point is the Banquet H which due to the genealogical painted on the wall is also called Habsburger Room.

400 meters above the Inn Valley is **Lake Achen**, Tyrol's largest and most beautiful lake. The stunningly cold water lends itself more to sailing and surfing than swimming. Ferries are in regular service all along the nine-kilometer long lake.

No other Tyrolean valley can compare in popularity to the **Ziller Valley (Zillertal)**. The **Zillertal Railw (Zillertalbahn)**, which opened in 1912, takes you from Jenbach to Mayrhofen (32 km) in a little less than hour. During the summer, the train is pulled twice daily by an old steam locomotive.

The Ziller Valley is also well-known for its friendly inhabitants and their local costumes as well as the valley's beautiful farmhouses, made completely of wood.

The Ziller River is the border between the Tyrolean and Salzburg diocese. On one side, the church towers are red, on the other, green.

The Ziller Valley remains wide and almost flat as far as **Mayrhofen**, then it divides into four gorgelike branches, of which only the Tuxer Valley is settled and "civilized" with tourist attractions. There is one village at the entrance to the Zillergrund, **Brandberg**.

The Hintertux glacier sweeps imposingly behind **Lanersbach** in the Tux Valley.

Spring or summer in the valley, eternal winter in the high mountains. Through the Ziller Valley glacier cablecar, the glacial regions of the **Gefrorene Wand** are a little nearer, even for those not in physical condition.

ɪg on the glacier, one gazes up to the 3476 meter-high **Olperer**.

Near Kramsach, halfway betw
Innsbruck and Kufstein, are th
small and charming lakes, nes
into meadows and forests, a
open to the public for swimming:
**Berglstein, Krumm and Rein
Lakes**. This is also where
Brandenberg Valley, a high va
still largely untouched, with the
pressive Kaiserklamm, conne
with the Inn Valley.

Alpbach, one of the prettiest villages of Tyrol, lies in the Alpbach valley, a southerly side valley of the main Lower Inn Valley. The entire area of this nucleated village is rich in farmhouses constructed as square houses, in part with chapels built of wood. Even today the characteristic local building traditions are respected and followed. Alpbach was first referred to officially in the middle of the 12th century and rose to prominence through mining and alpine dairy farming. Its Conference Centre has been home to the "European Forum Alpbach" for decades: lectures, discussions and exhibitions are intended to contribute to increased understanding between nations.

Also in Kramsach is the **open-air Museum Tyrolean Farmhouses (Museum Tiro Bauernhöfe)**, a wide expanse of meado on which farmhouses from all over Ty including their adjoining farm buildings s as grainhouses, mills, sawmills and smith all fully equipped, have been reconstructed

the entrance to the Alpbach Valley is the late Gothic **Burg Matzen** in the middle of a lush castle park. For ong time it was the residence of the rich mine owners of the lower Inn Valley: the Fiegers, and later, the ggers.

The charming little medieval city of **Rattenberg**, on the right bank of the Inn, squeezed in between the fortress on the hill and the river, was designed and built at the high point of the mining era in the 15th and 16th centuries.

In the northern end of the city is the former **Augustinian monastery**, in which a museum is housed today. Rattenberg and Kramsach are old glass-producing towns, and they continue their tradition to this day.

North of the Inn, on the terraces of the Angerberg, is **Mariastein**. Originally a higher, more massive tower belonging to the Lords of Freundsberg, it has been a highly popular place of pilgrimmage since the 15th century.

The **citadel** from the year 1200 dominates the view of **Kufstein**. Maximilian I. had the massive round structure built as an impregnable fortress in 1518-22.

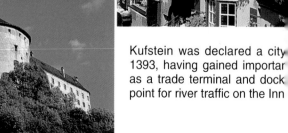

Kufstein was declared a city 1393, having gained importan as a trade terminal and dock point for river traffic on the Inn

ortheast of Kufstein, on the "Gentle Emperor" (Zahmen aiser) is the **Walchsee**. In the village of the same name, row of lower Inn Valley midfield houses with elaborately inted facades has been beautifully kept.

The overpowering gray walls of the **"Wild Empero** **(Wilder Kaiser)** at 2344 meters altitude, is the focus the whole region around St. Johann. The wealth lovely old houses in **St. Johann**, often with rich orn mentation or painted facades, is remarkable.

The medieval city plan of **Kitzbühel** is dominated by three and four story houses. During the 16th centu the city reached its historical high point after the d covery of silver and copper deposits. Since its very fi ski race in 1894, Kitzbühel has been a well-known wi ter resort, which has now found a summer counterp in popular tennis tournaments.

Two kilometers outside Kitzbühel, marshy **Black Lake (Schwarzsee)**, covered with water lilies, beckons the pleasures of a swim against the splendid backdrop of the Wild Emperor (Wilder Kaiser).

uite distinct from the touristic attractions of Kitzbühel is still splendidly bucolic **East Tyrol**. This is partly due its isolation, no doubt: since South Tyrol was ceded to Italy in 1919, there is no longer a direct route tween East Tyrol and its capital, Innsbruck, in North Tyrol. East Tyrol is even more mountainous than the st of Tyrol, demanding hard work of its farmers on the steep meadows of the **Lesach Valley**.

The **Felbertauern Tunnel** - here the south portal - connects East Tyrol with North Tyrol via the province of Salzburg.

Matrei in East Tyrol is the starting point for excursions into the Hohe Tauern, which is full of sporting and other leisure attractions. Matrei also has one of the most important examples of sacred architecture in the state: the tiny and inconspicuous **Nikolauskirche**. It is a Romanesque chancel-tower church, in which two chancels, one over the other, are housed in the massive tower. The frescoes from the 13th century are the most significant Romanesque paintings in the whole province of Tyrol.

The Virgen Valley leads round Matrei to the west and into the mountain massif of the Großvenediger. **Virgen**, the main village of the valley, boasts a very mild climate, despite its altitude of 1200 meters.

Among the sights of Virgen is the **pilgrimmage church Maria-Schnee in Obermauern**. The colorful and well-preserved frescoes in the church interior by Simon von Taisten, from the end of the 15th century, are its high point.

At the foot of the Virgen Valley in the middle of the planned National Park Hohe Tauern are the picturesqu **Umbal Waterfalls (Umbalfälle)**. Since 1978, visitors can see them close-up by means of the first waterfa observation path on the continent of Europe.

From Lienz one travels via the Isel Valley into the high-altitude Kalser Valley and then to the foot of the 3798 meter high **Großglockner**. The classic route to the summit of the highest mountain in Austria begins in Kals.

One of the oldest churches in the state is **St. Georg near Kals**, a tiny, archaic church in the middle of mountain meadows, far away from the hubbub of civilization. It was built in 1200. Excavations have brought to light discoveries dating back to the Roman era.

The **Defereggen Valley** is the biggest side valley on the Isel River and the best known valley in East Tyrol due to its beauty. On a sunny northern slope is **St. Veit**, at 1495 meters altitude the highest resort in Austria

enz is the biggest town in East
Tirol, with 13,000 inhabitants. It
is the economic heart of the
region. The **main square** radiates
warm through its floral
magnificence and street cafés,
giving the scene a real
Mediterranean flair.

The **parish church St. Andrä**, a
single-nave Gothic basilica is on a
rise, somewhat outside of town on
the far bank of the Isel. Three
earlier structures occupied the
same spot: a small early Christian
basilica from the 5th century, a
structure from the 9th-10th centuries and a Romanesque church.

The biggest attraction of Lienz,
however, is **Bruck Castle**, with its
massive tower, built on a steep
rock precipice. From here the
Counts of Görz were masters of
the crossing over the Isel from the

year 1280. Of artistic significance is
the chapel (Dreifaltigkeitskapelle)
decorated with wonderful frescoes
painted by Simon von Taisten in
1490.

About four kilometers from Lienz are the excavations of the Roma
city of Aguntum, which was declared a city by Emperor Claudius
the first century A.D. and became an important commercial cente
On the other side of the valley, about eight kilometers from Lienz,
the **Lavanter Kirchbichl**. Here the late follow-up settlement
Roman Aguntum has been excavated. Foundations, columns ar
altar have all been removed from the episcopal church.

the Puster Valley, a-
ove the entrance to the
llgraten Valley, the **Burg
einfels** stands en-
roned. This powerful
rtress belonged to the
ounts of Görz in the 13th
entury, and was ex-
anded in 1500. Today it
privately owned.

eneath the fortress, the
un Bridge spans the Vill-
aten brook. This 66 me-
r long, completely cov-
ed wooden bridge is the
dest and most beautiful
Tyrol.

The **Villgraten Valley** has its source in the Defereggen mountain massif. Of all the valleys in East Tyrol, this is still the most untouched. The mountain peaks are dense and bear down upon the high and isolated farm-houses, built on the uppermost meadows. The Vill-graten Valley is still full of sumptuous alms, lying in front of a heavily forested mountain backdrop. There are brooks full of trout, waterfalls, little lakes and a splendid selection of plants and animals.

The **Lesach Valley**, today also called the Tyrolean Gail Valley, stretches south from Sillian. It is the highest valley in East Tyrol.

In a valley clearing at 1450 meters altitude is **Obertilliach**, center of the Lesach Valley. Obertilliach has been able to preserve its old character so well that it has been declared a national monument. Between the remarkable East Tyrolean farmhouses are stables, grain stores and accompanying buildings just as they were hundreds of years ago.

Northwest of Innsbruck, between the Karwendel to the east, the Mieming Massif to the west and the **Wetterstein Massif** to the north is a small mountain plateau, the **Seefeld Plateau**.

At its center is **Seefeld**, 1180 meters, surrounded by forest-covered hills and the Wildsee.

As a winter resort, Seefeld places its focus not on alpine but nordic skiing. During the summer, Seefe

veals its countless hiking paths and the biggest (and most beautiful) **golf course** in Austria.

e landmark of Seefeld is the romantic little **lake church (Seekirchlein)**, a pretty Baroque structure ilt in 1628 by Christoph Gumpp the Younger, with a crucifix from the 16th century. The lake, on whose inks the church originally stood, has long since been transformed into meadows.

The view from Seefeld out over the **Hohe Munde** is at its best at sundown.

The **Leutasch Valley** stretches from the base of the Hohe Munde along the southern flank of the Wetterstein Massif as far as the German border. The scattered settlements - there are no fewer than 23 different village sections - spread throughout the entire valley, full of lovely old farmhouses and a special type of peasant painting known as "Lüftlmalerei." It is the longest village in Tyrol.

From Kematen in the Inn Valley, one enters the quiet mountain valley called Sellrain. At the end of the valley, one comes to the sun paradise **Kühtai**, above the tree line in the middle of high meadows and on the edge of the **Finstertal Reservoir**.

62

Kühtai is a tourist area full of guaranteed snowy slopes for every category of skier all winter long.

A little further upriver in the Inn Valley is **Stams**, where one of the historically important monasteries in Austria is located. It was founded in 1273 by Count Meinhard II. of Görz-Tyrol and his wife and served as the burial vaults of Tyrolean princes until 1563. The entire monastery complex was rebuilt in the style of the High Baroque at the beginning of the 18th century. Johann Martin Gumpp and his son Georg Anton were also active in this renewal.

On the other side of the Inn, 300 meters above the valley, is the **Mieminger Plateau**, well-known as an especially sunny holiday area for families.

Further upstream, the **Oetz Valley** stretches 65 kilometers to the south in five terraces, each at a higher altitude. On the second valley terrace, near Umhausen, are the **Stuiben Waterfalls**, which tumble 150 meters down into the valley. In **Umhausen**, the rich window frames and facade paintings catch the eye.

For alpinists, the Oetztal A
offer wonderful tours a
climbs: for example the c
pictured here, up the 376
meter high **Wildspitze**.

In 1991, on a high alpine h
over the Hauslab ridge
couple from Nuremberg fou
a corpse in the glacier ice
proved to be a sensatio
discovery. **"Oetzi"** as t
man became known to t
locals, is 5200 years old a
in astonishingly good conditi

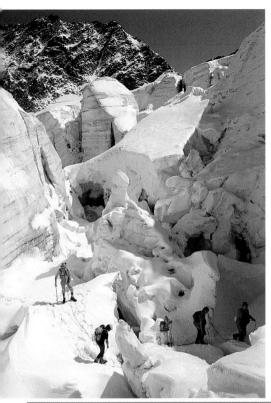

What could "Oetzi" have been looking for up in the glacier world on the **Similaun**, near the Finailspitze? These and other related questions occupy the scientists at Innsbruck University.

Not far from Imst, the **Pitz Valley** meets the Inn Valley. The Pitz Valley also stretches deep into the glac
terrain of the Oetztal Alps. It is the starting point for many spectacular mountain tours.

Imst, at the foot of the Lechtal Alps, like most of the alluvial hills of the upper Inn Valley, was an early settlement area. This figure of someone at prayer stems from the **Rhaetians**, who dominated the alpine region long before it was conquered by the Romans. During the Roman era and in the Middle Ages, Imst was an important crossroads. In the 15th century, mining in the area reached its high point.

The **"Schemen" ritual celebration of Imst** is one of the grandest Mardi Gras pre-fasting season festivals in the upper Inn Valley. It takes place only once every four years.

69

For thousands of years, long-distance routes coming from the Engadin, the Reschen Pass and the Arlbe have all joined the Inn Valley at Landeck. **Burg Landeck** stands proudly on a jutting rock pinnacle high ov the valley floor. It was originally built as castle for the judicial court, already referred to in documents of 129 Today it houses a local culture museum.

The upper Inn Valley reaches far into the impressive mountain world of the main chain of Alps. In the val below are the villages of **Prutz** and **Kauns**.

ve hundred meters above the Inn Valley stretches a high geological terrace known as the Sonnenterrasse. ere the well-known winter resorts of Serfaus, Ladis and Fiss are found.

esides skiing, **Serfaus** also has two parish churches. One of them **(Unsere liebe Frau im Walde)** is one of e oldest pilgrimmage churches in Tyrol.

oove the village of **Ladis, Burg Laudeck** stands enthroned, where for three hundred years the Prince's rator had his seat.

ke Ladis, **Fiss** is a typical Rhaeto-Roman settlement with fine houses built very close to one another, corated with pretty oriel windows and carved gables.

Southwest of Landeck, the valley of the Trisanna River, the **Paznaun**, branches off. It stretches into the southwestern corner of the state, all the way to the Silvretta High Alpine Road, a toll-road beginning at **Galtür** and only open during the summer. Ischgl is a popular winter resort; Ernest Hemingway loved Galtür; and **Mathon** is meditatively quiet.

When one leaves Landeck to the west, the Stanz Valley leads straight to the Arlberg and the pass separating Tyrol from Vorarlberg. Here is **St. Anton**, the birthplace of alpine skiing, with 200 km of meticulously kept ski slopes, including many for magnificent deep powder skiing. In summer, long and beautiful hikes can be undertaken in the whole region: for example, near **Schnann**.

The **Lech Valley** is connec
to the rest of Tyrol only via F
Pass and the town of Reu
Perhaps that's the reason
still so untouched. The L
River has been spared river
directing and leveling and to
is the last remaining wild r
landscape in the Eastern Alp

Especially the side valleys of the Lech - here, the **Bschlabser Valley** - are still very primeval, with their woodblock houses, built completely without nails. Woodworking was always an important sideline occupation of the Lechtal farmers. Woodcarving is still practiced today. The houses of **Elbigenalp** are ornamented with marvellous paintings and stucco decorations.

A side valley of the Lechtal is the **Tannheimer Valley**. The whole valley floor is filled by Lake Halder encircled by meadows and stretches of forest.

eutte is the main town of the Ausserfern region, an important crossroads. The impressive bourgeois ouses of the town bear witness to the fact that Reutte reached a high degree of wealth from the salt trade uring the Middle Ages. In the vicinity of Reutte are two lakes, connected with each other by a canal, **Lake an and Lake Heiterwanger**.

Shortly beyond Fern Pass, at the foo
the massive south wall of the **Zugspi**
is **Ehrwald**, the best point of access
the highest mountain summit in G
many and the point of departure for
Zugspitzbahn, the cablecar up to
heights.

rn Pass stretches through a mountainous forest landscape, spotted with tiny lakes, such as idyllic **Lake rnstein**.

We hope that in this picture book we have succeeded in bringing the reader a little closer to the most valuable asset of the "Land in the Mountains" - namely, the incomparable grandeur of the mountain landscape and the picturesque beauty of the villages whose culture is still ever-present and an integral part of everyday life to its people. Perhaps the accents which we touched upon in these pictures will inspire you to get to know the "Heart of the Alps" all the way into its deepest valleys.